HOW TO AMAZE YOUR SON

A Firefly Book

Published by Firefly Books Ltd. 2015

English translation copyright © 2015 Firefly Books
Original publication © 2014 Tana éditions, an imprint of Édi8

First printing

Publisher Cataloging-in-Publication Data (U.S.)

Vidaling, Raphaële.
   How to amaze your son : crafts, recipes and other creative experiences to teach him to see the extraordinary in the ordinary / Raphaële Vidaling.
First English edition.
Originally published by Tana Editions, Paris, France as Comment épater son fils.
[144] pages : color photographs ; cm.
Includes index.
Summary: "A collection of crafts for boys that take ordinary items to make them extraordinary"– Provided by publisher.
ISBN-13: 978-1-77085-602-8 (pbk.)
1. Handicraft. 2. Recipes. I. Title.
745.5 dc23   TT171.V533 2015

Library and Archives Canada Cataloguing in Publication

Vidaling, Raphaële
[Comment épater son fils. English]
   How to amaze your son : crafts, recipes and other creative experiences to teach him to see the extraordinary in the ordinary / Raphaële Vidaling.
Includes index.
Translation of: Comment épater son fils.
ISBN 978-1-77085-602-8 (paperback)
   1. Handicraft for boys. 2. Creative activities and seat work.
3. Parent and child. I. Title. II. Title: Comment épater son fils. English
TT157.V5313 2015   745.5083   C2015-903759-X

Published in the United States by
Firefly Books (U.S.) Inc.
P.O. Box 1338, Ellicott Station
Buffalo, New York 14205

Published in Canada by
Firefly Books Ltd.
50 Staples Avenue, Unit 1
Richmond Hill, Ontario L4B 0A7

Printed in China

Conceived, designed, and produced
by Tana éditions, an imprint of d'Édi8
12, avenue d'Italie
75013 Paris
www.tana.fr

How to Amaze Your Son

CRAFTS, RECIPES AND OTHER CREATIVE EXPERIENCES
TO TEACH HIM TO SEE THE EXTRAORDINARY IN THE ORDINARY

TEXT, PHOTOS AND DESIGN
RAPHAËLE VIDALING

FIREFLY BOOKS

INTRODUCTION

"All children are artists. The problem is how to remain an artist once he grows up." This sentence is Picasso's. But what is an artist? Someone who looks at the world with a curious eye, gifted with a creativity that transforms raw material into poetry? Yes, children have this talent, this perpetual wonder that makes them enthusiastic for new experiences, capable of investing themselves in a little project with as much enthusiasm and seriousness as they would if their life depended on it: making soap bubbles or paper airplanes, tying a remote-control motor to a stuffed animal on wheels, or making a skirt of flowers to put around a little doll. Playing is about inventing, testing, letting your imagination and concrete experiences rub up against one another. And, in the end, it's about growing as well. Only while growing up, we sometimes lose our open mind. We throw out bottle caps without seeing the possibility of them being wheels: we no longer pick up feathers on the sidewalk. Sometimes, even, we forget to sculpt volcanoes in our mashed potatoes! That is, we forget unless we have the chance to have children of our own, who remind us not to neglect the most important things: play, fantasy and making wonderful things for the sake of making something wonderful!

This book is a helping hand for parents who haven't lost their inner child, for those who, between the "brush your teeth" and "don't forget to say thank you" will add the essential insight: "Never forget to see the extraordinary in the ordinary!"

TABLE OF CONTENTS

82. EXPERIMENTS AND MAGIC TRICKS

104. AND YOU CAN EAT IT!

ACTIVITIES
to do together

A 3D HAND
THAT'S EASY TO DRAW

MATERIALS
A SHEET OF PAPER
A PENCIL
MARKERS OF DIFFERENT COLORS
AN ERASER

HOW TO MAKE

1. Place your hand on the sheet of paper and trace it with a pencil.

2. With a marker, draw a horizontal line anywhere on the sheet of paper, starting at the edge of the page and continuing toward the middle until it reaches the edge of the traced hand outline. Next, extend the marker line through the tracing, but make a gentle arc from one traced edge to the other. When you reach the other edge of the tracing, continue the line – completely straight – to the other edge of the page.

3. Draw more lines parallel to the first one, including the arc, until you've filled your sheet with multicolored stripes.

4. Erase the pencil lines: Now the hand appears without the traced outline and looks 3D.

Trace your hand.

Draw curved lines inside the tracing
to create the 3D illusion.

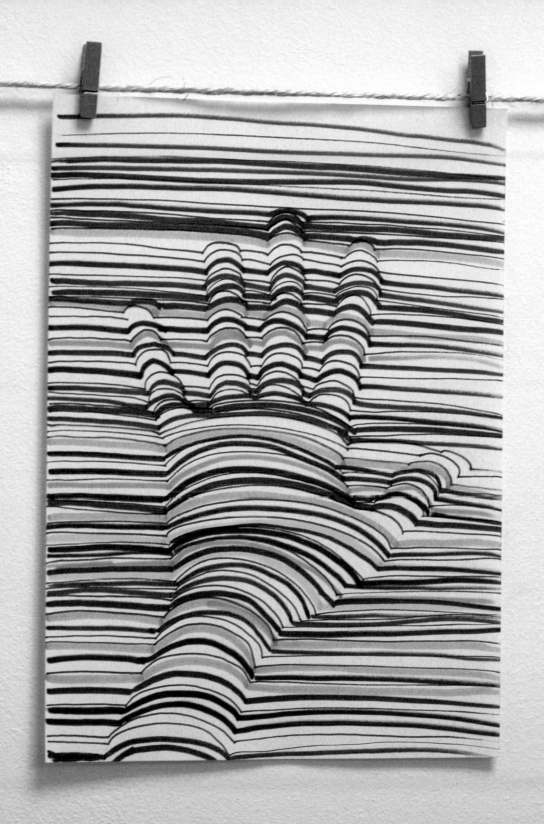

11

LITTLE MEN
MADE FROM SPROUTED POTATOES

MATERIALS
SPROUTED POTATOES
WHITE CORRECTION FLUID
A BLACK MARKER
MATCHES

HOW TO MAKE

1 Draw eyes and a mouth on each potato with the correction fluid.

2 When the correction fluid is dry, use the black marker to add the other details.

3 Insert matches into the potatoes to create the feet.

A STAR BOX
MADE FROM A COLA BOTTLE

HOW TO MAKE

1 Using the box cutter, cut the bottle into two sections so you end up with a bottom half that is a bit shorter than the top half.

2 With your scissors, cut out a vertical notch in every second groove of the bottle, for a total of five, cutting down to where the bottom of the bottle starts to get bigger.

3 Cut out petal shapes from those five bands. Fold back one petal toward the inside. Repeat for all five petals and the box is done!

4 To decorate, apply glue to the bottle and cover with tissue paper.

MATERIALS

A BOX CUTTER
A LARGE (67.6 FL. OZ [2 L]) COLA BOTTLE
SCISSORS
WHITE GLUE
A GLUE BRUSH
TISSUE PAPER OR PAPER NAPKINS

Like magic – it stays shut on its own!

When fully open, it acts as a vase.

Children can decorate it on their own using torn tissue paper.

If using paper napkins, only use the top layer that has the designs on it.

15

TURNING A WALK INTO ART
SIMPLE AND FREE

MATERIALS
FEET FOR WALKING
HANDS FOR PICKING THINGS UP
EYES TO SEE
A CAMERA

HOW TO MAKE
1 Take a walk. Pick up little things from the ground.
2 Carefully place them next to each other until you're happy with the arrangement.
3 Take a photo of the assembled objects, then resume your walk.

RETOUCHED PHOTOS
OR WHAT IF WE DREW ON MY LITTLE BROTHER?

MATERIALS
A BABY
A WHITE SHEET
A CAMERA
A PRINTER
A BLACK MARKER

HOW TO MAKE
1 Lay the baby down on the white sheet.
2 Take full-body photos, with the baby awake or asleep in various positions.
3 Print the photos (or have them printed).
4 Draw on the photos with the marker.

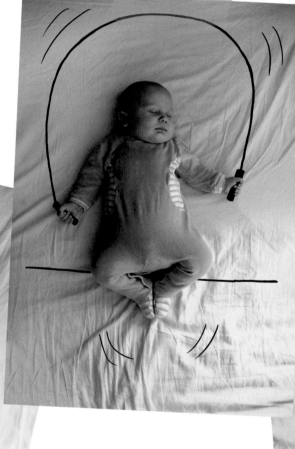

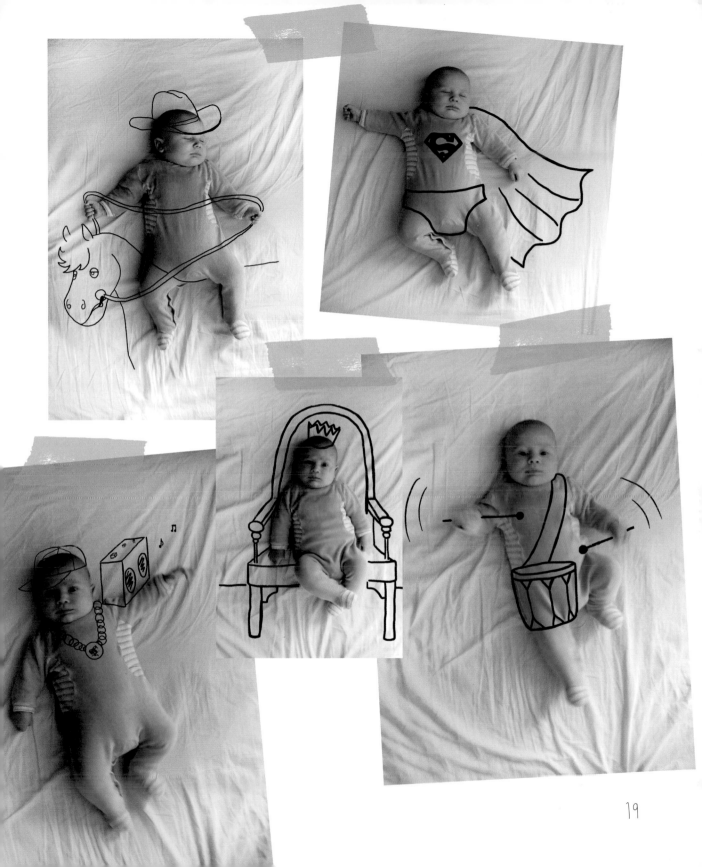

THE ART OF KOKEDAMA
HANGING JAPANESE GARDENS
苔玉

Even a simple daisy can transform into a UFO to hang in your room.

MATERIALS
MODELING CLAY
SMALL PLANTS
POTTING SOIL
PEAT SOIL
SPHAGNUM MOSS
A LARGE BOWL
SOLID BLACK THREAD
FINE METAL WIRE

HOW TO MAKE

1 Soak the modeling clay in water for a few hours so it will soften.

2 While you're waiting, go for a walk, dig up some small plants and collect some patches of moss. Or visit a garden center for these materials.

3 Mix one-third modeling clay, one-third potting soil and one-third peat soil in the bowl to create a uniform and workable paste.

4 Delicately loosen the soil from the roots of your chosen plant.

5 Form a ball of paste around the roots, then wrap with moss.

6 Hold everything together by thoroughly wrapping the sphere with thread, and then make a knot.

7 Fasten the metal wire to the thread or through the sphere so the plant can be hung. Mist with water or submerge the plant in water from time to time.

If you add small figurines, you can create the planets from *The Little Prince.*

AN ALPHABETICAL SHELF
MADE FROM YOGURT CONTAINERS

HOW TO MAKE

1 Using a pencil, trace the placement of the containers on the cardboard.

2 Cut out the holes with a box cutter.

3 Glue the rims of the containers onto the cardboard.

4 Using a white marker, write the letters of the alphabet onto the cardboard.

5 Fill the compartments with small objects that have names that begin with the letter that corresponds to the letter over the slot.

MATERIALS
TWENTY-SIX YOGURT CONTAINERS
   (OR OTHER CONTAINERS WITH A RIM)
CARDBOARD
A PENCIL
A BOX CUTTER
GLUE
A WHITE MARKER

Seen from the back. This is a small do-it-yourself project to work on together, which costs nothing to make.

A good exercise to learn
about letters and
to put things away!

23

BALLS OF ICE
LIT FROM THE INSIDE

MATERIALS
BALLOONS
WATER
TEA LIGHTS

HOW TO MAKE

1 Thread the opening of a balloon to a faucet and fill the balloon with water. Tie the balloon shut and knot it.

2 Leave the balloon in the freezer until the next day.

3 Take the balloon out of the freezer: after one night, the center of the ball should not have fully frozen and there should still be liquid inside. Rip the balloon and empty the water.

4 The result is a magnificent translucent sphere. Place one of the tea lights in the center.

24

When night falls
they look
really beautiful.

In wintertime,
when it stays very cold,
you can light up a walkway
in your yard.

26

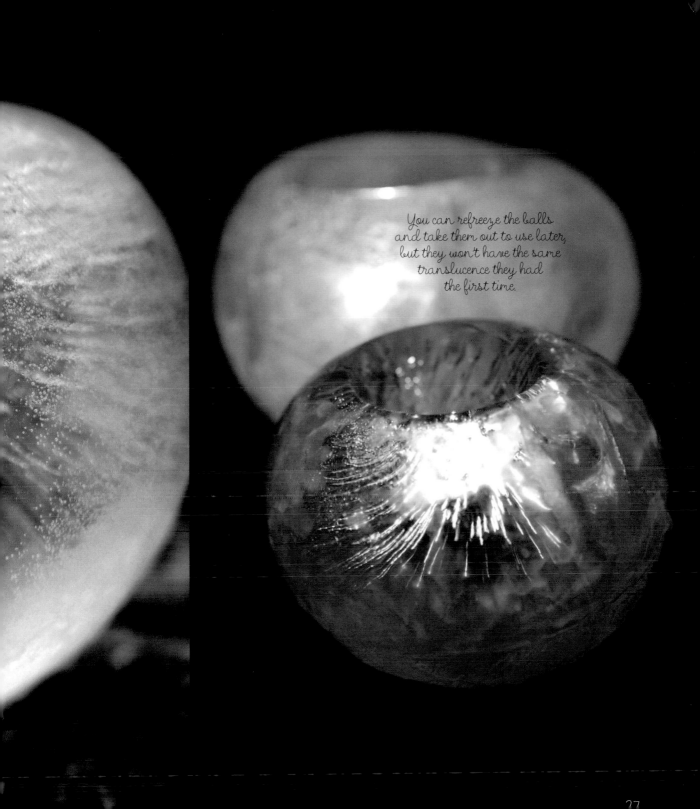

You can refreeze the balls
and take them out to use later,
but they won't have the same
translucence they had
the first time.

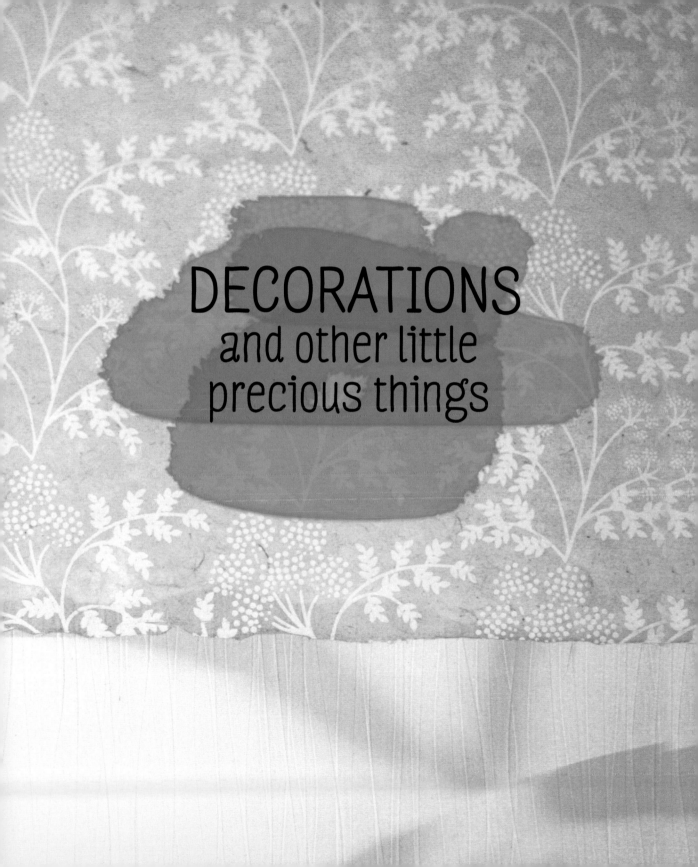

DECORATIONS
and other little precious things

A SMALL, MYSTERIOUS DOOR
THAT HIDES AN ELECTRICAL OUTLET

MATERIALS

FOAM CORE BOARD
  (ABOUT THE SAME THICKNESS AS THE OUTLET)
A PIECE OF THIN CARDBOARD
SCISSORS
GLUE
A PIECE OF FABRIC
A SMALL WOODEN FRUIT CRATE
A BRASS FASTENER
A DRILL WITH A SMALL BIT
STRING
WOOD STAIN
DOUBLE-SIDED ADHESIVE TAPE

HOW TO MAKE

1 Cut out two door shapes from the foam core board and one from the thin cardboard.

2 Make a hole that's the same size as the wall outlet in one of the foam core board cutouts, and a hole the same size as the plug in the thin cardboard. Glue the thin cardboard onto the foam core board cutout.

3 Join the two doors by gluing the piece of fabric to both doors to act as a hinge.

4 Cut out small slats from the crate with scissors. Glue them onto the cardboard.

5 Make a hole in the door and insert the brass fastener into it to create a door handle.

6 Cut out small slats from the crate. Drill tiny holes into them and thread the string, knotting it under each step, to construct the ladder.

7 Cut out a small landing the width of the door, drill some holes to attach the ladder and then glue it to the bottom of the doorframe.

8 Stain the wood (you can also use diluted paint or shoe polish).

9 Attach the door to the wall using pieces of double-sided adhesive tape.

A wooden version with hinges and a staircase made of fruit crate slats.

A FLYING FISH
MADE FROM A SPROUTED ONION

MATERIALS
A SPROUTED ONION
A FINE MARKER
WHITE CORRECTION FLUID
TOOTHPICK
STRING
A BEAD
ADHESIVE TAPE

HOW TO MAKE

1 Use the marker and correction fluid to draw the eye and the scales of the fish onto the onion.

2 Pierce the onion from the top to the bottom with the toothpick and thread the string through the hole (to help with the stringing, you can attach the thread to the toothpick with a piece of adhesive tape). Knot the end of the thread to a bead situated under the fish.

3 Suspend the fish like a mobile. Its tail will continue to grow!

A BOOK WITH A SECRET HIDING PLACE
THAT DATES BACK TO A TIME OF REAL TREASURES

HOW TO MAKE

1 To create a box with a good depth, use two books glued together. To make them look more natural, don't align them perfectly on top of one another. Start with the smaller book, which will be on top. Using a pencil, mark the placement of the hole on the back of the book, and then cut the back cover with your box cutter.

2 Extend the cutting into the interior pages, but don't cut through the front pages – these should be left intact.

3 Place the small book on top of the bigger one, mark the outline of the hole with the pencil, then cut out the front cover of the bigger book, followed by the inside pages.

4 Glue the two books together, then glue a band of cardboard around the edges of the hole. Cover the cardboard with decorative paper.

MATERIALS

TWO OLD USED BOOKS
A PENCIL
A BOX CUTTER
A RULER
THIN CARDBOARD
DECORATIVE PAPER
GLUE

A PEANUT TROPHY
FOR VEGETARIAN HUNTERS

MATERIALS
A SMALL LOG
A SAW
SOME METAL WIRE
A NAIL
A HAMMER
SHELLED PEANUTS
A KNIFE
GLUE
MARKERS

HOW TO MAKE

1 Saw off a round portion from the log. Form a small bow with the metal wire and nail it to the back of the cut-off piece so you can hang your trophy on the wall when it is complete.

2 Choose a shelled peanut that looks like it will make the best reindeer head. Cut it with your knife to keep only part of the shell. You might need to do this several times before it looks just right!

3 Using a marker, draw the eyes and the mouth on the peanut shell.

4 Glue the shell onto the round piece of log.

5 Draw the antlers and ears.

6 Hang the trophy above a fireplace or over your bed.

A FRUIT CRATE TREE HOUSE
PERCHED IN A STALK OF BROCCOLI

MATERIALS

TWO HEADS OF BROCCOLI
   (ONE FULL HEAD + ONE STEM)
SCISSORS
A WOODEN FRUIT CRATE
TOOTHPICKS
STRING
GLUE
A KNIFE
WOODEN SKEWERS

HOW TO MAKE

1 Choose the best spot on the head of broccoli where you'll attach the tree house. Using scissors, cut the terrace, which will come out of the stem, out of a piece of wooden crate. Insert some toothpicks into the stem; these will be used to support the house.

2 Make some holes in the terrace and insert some toothpicks. Interlace some string to create a railing.

3 Cut out some thin slats from the crate and build the three walls of the house (with windows and doors), glued on the vertical supports. Glue the walls onto the terrace. Glue on the roof and cover it with shingles – also made out of the crate slats.

4 Cut out a landing made from the crate and pierce it in three spots. Attach the full head of broccoli to the upside-down stem from the second head of broccoli, with the landing between them, using three pieces of wooden skewers pricked in and passing through the holes. Add the terrace support beams, made out of skewers.

5 Cut the stairs into points. Create slits in the broccoli stem and insert the stairs.

A person made out of a brass fastener and bamboo.

The tree house only has three sides. It's built to come out of the stem.

The installation of the deck, landing and spiral staircase.

38

Tip to raise the height of the trunk: There are two broccoli stems — the bottom one has been placed upside down.

39

A SHARK PENCIL CASE
WITH METAL TEETH

MATERIALS

A PIECE OF FABRIC MEASURING 8X60 INCHES
    (20X150 CM)
FABRIC SCRAPS FOR THE LINING
SCISSORS
TWO EYES (MADE OF BUTTONS OR GLUED ON)
A NEEDLE AND THREAD
SILVER MARKER (OPTIONAL)
A SEWING MACHINE
A 6-INCH (15-CM) LONG METAL ZIPPER

HOW TO MAKE

1 Cut out the pieces as indicated on the pattern. For the lining, you'll only need the underside piece and the two parts of the back.

2 Sew or glue on the eyes. Embroider the gills or draw them on with a silver marker.

3 Sew (inside out) the elements that will create the fin and the flippers in pairs.

4 Sew together (inside out) the two top pieces that imbed the fin in the middle of the back. Also sew the end of the tail on the corresponding bottom piece, keeping it inside out.

5 Sew the zipper on the back and belly sides.

6 Sew the sides, imbedding the flippers into the seam, all the way to the tail.

7 Turn your shark right side out and finish by hand the joining of the tail and the back (approximately 1¼ inches [3 cm]).

8 Create the lining by assembling the three parts like a small bag, then sew this by hand.

Tip for less experienced sewers: find a used stuffed animal, empty it out and add the zipper.

41

MINIATURE CHAIRS
MADE FROM CHAMPAGNE CAPS

—ᗰᗰ—

HOW TO MAKE

1 Cut the metal wire at the bottom of the cork cage by opening, with pliers, what will become the chair legs.

2 Use the available wire to create a chair back.

3 Attach the two ends of the chair back wire to the rear legs of the chair, and repeat these steps for all the corks, varying the shapes of the chair backs.

MATERIALS

TOPS WITH CAPS AND CAGES (FROM CHAMPAGNE OR MOCK-CHAMPAGNE BOTTLES)
LONG NOSE PLIERS

Start a pretty collection that will remind you of the holidays.

A variation on the chair, with arm rests.

A DRUM KIT
MADE FROM SMALL TIN CANS

MATERIALS

TWO SMALL TIN CANS OF THE SAME SIZE
ONE BIG TIN CAN
ONE MEDIUM AND FLAT TIN CAN
   (LIKE A CAN OF TUNA)
ONE SMALL AND TALL TIN CAN
A CAN OPENER
A NAIL
A HAMMER
METAL WIRE
PLIERS

A tripod: turn each bow into a coil and twist the ends onto the pole.

HOW TO MAKE

1 Open, empty, wash and dry all the cans. Or use cans saved from your recycling bin.

2 Pierce the middle of each lid of each of the three smallest cans with your nail and hammer.

3 Create drum stands with the metal wire, doubled and coiled with your pliers.

4 Place the cans on their stands and secure the pierced can lid cymbals onto the poles of the tripods.

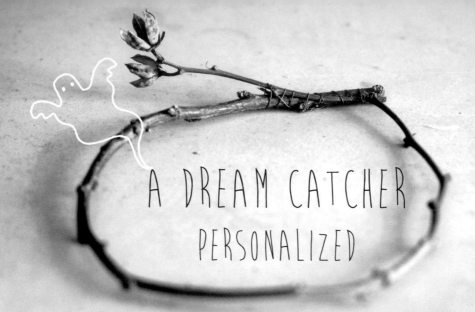

A DREAM CATCHER
PERSONALIZED

HOW TO MAKE

1 Form a circle with the branch and keep it in place with the thin metal wire.

2 Tie the string anywhere on the circle and twist it loosely all around the branch. Tie the end of the string at the starting point.

3 Tie another piece of string to the middle of a segment of the first piece of string, then tie it to the middle of the second segment, etc. until you have returned to the starting point.

4 Proceed in the same way with multiple pieces of string, making them shorter and shorter until you reach the center. Fasten the large bead in the middle.

5 Attach small objects with thread to the bottom of the dream catcher: these objects are what give the dream catcher its value as a talisman.

6 Hang the dream catcher over your bed to filter out nightmares. According to Native legends, the bad dreams will get stuck in the net and will burn at the first sign of dawn.

MATERIALS

A THIN, FLEXIBLE BRANCH
THIN METAL WIRE
STRING
THREAD
ONE BIG BEAD
SMALL OBJECTS
    (PERSONAL AND WELL-LOVED)

Step 3: the second piece of string is tied to the coil that was created by the first piece.

TWO KINDS OF SURPRISE BOXES
✸ THE DISGUISED CANS ✸

MATERIALS
A CAN OF SAUERKRAUT
A CAN OF BEANS
PAPER
SCISSORS
A PENCIL
ADHESIVE TAPE

HOW TO MAKE

1 Remove the labels from the cans and use them as a template. Place the labels on the sheet of paper. Draw an outline of each label and cut it out from the piece of paper to create the new labels.

2 Draw faces in proportion to the size of each can.

3 Wrap the new labels around the cans. Keep each label in place with the adhesive tape. Open the cans.

✷ A Box of Chocolates with no Chocolate ✷

MATERIALS
AN EMPTY ASSORTED CHOCOLATE BOX
COINS AND BILLS

HOW TO MAKE

1 Place the coins and the folded bills into the compartments that once held the chocolates.

2 Close the box. The recipient will be surprised by your gift!

A GHOST
MADE FROM STARCHED FABRIC

Using a balloon for the big ghost, and a clementine for the small one.

The two ghosts drying after the spray starch was applied.

MATERIALS

GAUZE OR CHEESECLOTH
SPRAY STARCH
    (AVAILABLE IN THE LAUNDRY AISLE)
A BALLOON
AN EMPTY GLASS BOTTLE
METAL WIRE
TWO DARK, LIGHTWEIGHT BEADS
THREAD
A NEEDLE

HOW TO MAKE

1 Create the underlying shape of the ghost by placing the balloon on top of the bottle and by bending the metal wire to shape its arms.

2 Cover the entire underlying shape with gauze or cheesecloth. If needed, wet the fabric to make it more flexible.

3 Thoroughly spray all sides with the spray starch. Let it dry near a heat source until the next day.

4 Carefully remove the ghost from its frame and sew on the beads where the eyes should go (you can also sew on buttons or glue on some black dots).

for
PLAYING

A MUMMY
CONTORTIONIST

MATERIALS
ELECTRICAL WIRE OR
    OTHER THIN METAL WIRE
CUTTING PLIERS
THIN WHITE FABRIC
SCISSORS

HOW TO MAKE

1 Create a small figure out of electrical wire (or metal wire).

2 Tear the white fabric into thin bands. To tear, start by making a small cut with your scissors and then pulling with both hands; the fabric will easily tear.

3 Cover the figure with bands of fabric, tying the fabric at the ends.

4 Bend your figure and place it in various positions.

A very simple model, with twisted limbs.

56

A TREE HOUSE
MADE OF CARDBOARD

The pieces all cut and ready. Easy to assemble once that's done!

The slide tube! Since you can't have a real one in your bedroom....

MATERIALS
CARDBOARD
BOX CUTTER AND SCISSORS
A PENCIL
STRING
GLUE
A PIECE OF NETTING
  (FROM A BAG OF POTATOES
  OR ONIONS)

HOW TO MAKE

1 Cut out three pieces of cardboard for the trunk, each measuring 24 inches (60 cm) high and approximately 6 inches (15 cm) wide. Cut out two circles measuring 16 inches (40 cm) in diameter for each story, then one measuring 18 inches (45 cm) for the base, and another measuring 28 inches (70 cm) for the roof. You can use cardboard scraps to cut out the landing (approximately 10 inches [25 cm] in diameter), the roof ornaments and the accessories.

2 Cut holes and a trapdoor in each story. Cut out a slit in the cardboard piece that will be used for the landing.

3 Create 2½-inch (6 cm) long slits into each tree trunk at the one-third mark and again at the two-thirds mark.

4 Mark three equidistant points on the circumference of the circles – which will become the stories – and create 3 -inch (8-cm) long slits towards the center. Test the assembly of the stories into the trunks and adjust the length of the slits, if needed.

5 Create the ladder, stairs, slide and tube out of the cardboard, as well as a ladder made of string. Assemble all the elements.

6 Cut out pieces of cardboard in the shape of leaves and glue them to the roof. Place the roof on top of the trunk and attach the net. Place the entire structure on the base. Invite some guests to come live in your tree house.

MULTICOLORED MADELEINES
MADE FROM WAX CRAYON ENDS

HOW TO MAKE

1 Remove the paper labels from the crayons. Break the crayons into small pieces. Divide the pieces between the silicone molds in the pan.

2 Place in the oven at 65°F (150°C) for 5 minutes to melt. If they haven't melted by that time, continue to bake until they do.

3 Remove the molds from the oven. You can use a sharp object to mix the colors together when the wax is still melted, but note that it hardens quickly. As soon as they've cooled, unmold your new crayons and start drawing…

MATERIALS
WAX CRAYON ENDS
SMALL SILICONE MOLD PAN

And you can draw with many colors at once

A way to recycle all the crayon ends that clutter up containers.

When melting, the colors mix together and create a beautiful surprise.

62

63

A TEEPEE
MADE FROM AN OLD SHEET

Time to play!

MATERIALS

AN OLD TWIN-SIZED SHEET
A PIECE OF FAUX SUEDE FABRIC MEASURING
   APPROXIMATELY 28×28 INCHES (70×70 CM)
SEWING SCISSORS
THREAD AND A SEWING MACHINE
SIX BAMBOO POLES, EACH MEASURING
   100 INCHES (250 CM) IN LENGTH
NINE SMALL WOODEN STICKS (OR WOODEN SKEWERS)
METAL WIRE
TWINE

HOW TO MAKE

1 Cut the sheet according to the diagram. You'll end up with five big triangles and two small ones. With this pattern you won't have to create a hem on the bottom or on the length of the front-facing flaps.

2 Sew the triangles together so they create a teepee (leaving 2 inches [5 cm] unsewn at the top). On the front-facing panel, sew together only part of the two panels (leave half the panel unsewn at the bottom, and 12 inches [30 cm] at the top). Sew over the bib, then make holes and thread the poles into the holes.

3 At the bottom of each seam joining the panels, sew a little pocket inside that will be used to thread the ends of the bamboo poles.

4 At the top, add two fabric triangles, create a hem with a vertical slit in the middle and thread two metal wires into the hem. The wires will come out of the hem and be used to secure the fabric to the bamboo poles that will be held together by a piece of twine, as well as to strengthen the wings of fabric, which you can position to your liking.

When the teepee is complete,
you can invite your friends.

AN ICE WREATH
FROM PREHISTORIC TIMES

MATERIALS
PLASTIC ANIMALS
A RING-SHAPED MOLD
WATER
SMALL HAMMER (OPTIONAL)

*Within each child there is
an archeologist, especially when
there's a chance to break some ice!*

HOW TO MAKE

1 Lay the animals in the mold.

2 Fill the mold almost to the top with water.

3 Place in the freezer and let set until the next day.

4 Unmold and hang outside on your front door or offer the wreath to children, who will free animals that are stuck in the ice with the help of a small hammer.

A BALLOON ROCKET
WITH A SECRET MESSAGE

Slide the message
inside the balloon.

The perfect device to join two rooms.

MATERIALS

A BALLOON
STRING
A STRAW
ADHESIVE TAPE
A SECRET MESSAGE WRITTEN
   ON PAPER
A CLAMP OR A HAIR BARRETTE
SCISSORS

HOW TO MAKE

1 Slide the tightly rolled message into the balloon. Blow up the balloon. Keep it shut with a clamp or a barrette, without making a knot.

2 Cut off the bendy part of the straw, if it has one, so you end up with a completely straight straw. Thread the string through the straw. Elongate the balloon, place the straw on top of it, in the middle, and attach it in place using two pieces of adhesive tape.

3 Stretch the string between the person sending the message (with the opening of the balloon toward them) and the person receiving it. When the string is fully extended, open the clamp and let go of the balloon: it will be propelled to the end of the string. All that's left to do is to deflate the balloon to retrieve the message.

A HOUSE UNDER THE TABLE
MADE WITH PAPER TABLECLOTHS

It's even prettier at night when you place a small lamp under the table...

... especially if you've cut out window holes and created glass using tracing paper!

MATERIALS

A TABLE
SEVERAL PAPER TABLECLOTHS
A MARKER
ADHESIVE TAPE
A MEASURING TAPE
SCISSORS

HOW TO MAKE

1 Measure the length and the width of the table.

2 Cut the paper tablecloths according to the measurements, covering three sides of the table.

3 Draw a door and windows with a marker.

4 Attach the panels of paper under the table with adhesive tape.

A TINY HOUSE
MADE FROM A GRAPEFRUIT

HOW TO MAKE

1 Cut off one-quarter of the grapefruit: it will serve as the roof.

2 Remove the pulp from both sections of the grapefruit, ensuring that only the white skin is left inside.

3 Cut out the door and the window, as well as a notch in the roof where the chimney will sit. Use the cut-out piece from the door to create the chimney by re-cutting it into a rectangle.

4 Finally, place the roof on the house.

5 You can dry the house out on a radiator or a sunny windowsill so that the skin hardens: the house will keep for a very long time if you do.

MATERIALS

ONE GRAPEFRUIT
A SHARP KNIFE
A SMALL SPOON

Choose your proportions well:
the small piece becomes the roof.

A variation – use kumquats to create
a family of tiny people.

73

THE GAME OF MOLKKY®
A CROSS BETWEEN BOWLING AND BOCCE

HOW TO MAKE

1 Use your saw to cut one 9-inch (22 cm), and twelve 6-inch (15 cm) long logs. Make sure they can stand on their own. If they don't, use the saw to level the bottoms.

2 Mark a number from 1 to 12 on each of the pins. Keep the tallest one blank — it will be used for throwing.

THE RULES OF THE GAME

This very popular Finnish game is played with many players, sometimes in teams. It's ideal at the beach — for children as well as adults.

Place the pins standing up and grouped according to the order visible on the photos. One by one, the players, positioned approximately 10 feet (3 m) away, throw the unmarked piece of wood at the pins. If a single pin is knocked over, the player wins the number of points that corresponds with the number written on the pin. If several pins are knocked over, the player wins as many points as the number of pins that have fallen.

The pins are set up again at the exact spot where the top of the pin had previously fallen. As a result, the pins will begin to spread out throughout the game.

The winner is the player who successfully accumulates exactly 50 points. If the player goes over this score, he or she will have their score immediately lowered to 25. Finally, in the case of three nil scores in a row, the player is eliminated.

MATERIALS

BRANCHES MEASURING 2½ INCHES (6 CM) IN DIAMETER (6½ FEET [2 M] IN TOTAL LENGTH)
A SAW OR CHAINSAW
A MARKER

Beach souvenirs. The real game has pins cut with beveled tops.

A CATAPULT
MADE FROM POPSICLE STICKS

Only takes a few minutes to make, but provides hours of fun afterward.

MATERIALS
EIGHT POPSICLE STICKS
SIX ELASTIC BANDS
A SMALL PLASTIC SPOON
CANDY TO BE USED AS PROJECTILES

HOW TO MAKE

1 Fasten four Popsicle sticks together with two elastic bands placed near the ends of the sticks (in orange on the photo).

2 Fasten together four more Popsicle sticks, this time only on one end of the sticks (in blue on the photo).

3 Keep the connection firmly secured by using two more elastic bands.

4 Attach the small spoon with an elastic band. To launch a projectile, press down on the spoon while securing the front of the catapult.

A JUNGLE CAVE
MADE WITH ROCK PAPER

HOW TO MAKE

1 Layer the reclaimed cardboard, cut up or in its entirety, to create many levels and openings on every side.

2 Cover the entire structure with rock paper. Crinkling the paper will give it a more authentic look. Glue it on.

3 Glue felt onto the board to represent grass, making holes where the ponds will be.

4 To create a pond, glue aluminum foil onto the board, squeeze some glue around the edge of the pond to create a ridge, and pour sand onto the glue, gently tapping it to help it stay in place.

5 Glue the cave onto the board before inviting the animals!

MATERIALS

MULTIPLE PIECES OF
   RECYCLED CARDBOARD
SCISSORS
ROCK PAPER
GREEN FELT
A LARGE BOARD
WHITE GLUE
A GLUE BRUSH
FINE SAND
ALUMINUM FOIL

To reinforce the cave, use a wooden crate for the base, screwing it into the board after you've created your openings with your jigsaw. This is what was done here.

79

The cave can also be used as
a garage, pirate hideaway, etc.

The little pond with
a sandy shore
is a nice feature
near this jungle
apartment.

EXPERIMENTS
and magic tricks

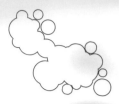

A LITTLE CHEMIST'S CRATERS
AN EXPERIMENT WITH BAKING SODA

The eruption is short-lived, but if you're the height of a small figurine, it's a volcano!

MATERIALS
WHITE VINEGAR
INKS
A FEW SMALL GLASSES
BAKING SODA
A DISH

HOW TO MAKE

1 Prepare small glasses of white vinegar, dying each with a different color of ink.

2 Spread some baking soda on the bottom of the dish.

3 Drop a few drops of the colored vinegar with the eyedropper and observe the chemical reaction. You'll end up with small, pretty halos of colored foam.

AN ICEBERG
MADE OF MICROWAVED SOAP

HOW TO MAKE

1 Place the soap, without the packaging, inside the microwave oven. Heat at maximum power for 30 seconds.

2 Repeat this step while observing every 30 seconds. The soap will swell at its optimal point at the end of approximately 90 seconds. After this amount of time, you risk browning the soap and having it fall flat.

3 Let the soap cool down. After a few minutes, the soap will have hardened and the foam will have become solid.

MATERIALS

A MICROWAVE OVEN
A BAR OF SOAP

Allow the soap to harden after 90 seconds of cooking time. Longer, and it will be too much!

At the 60-second mark: it swells; it foams and it smells!

The soap at the end of 30 seconds in the microwave. It's starting to move

87

A MAGICAL MERRY-GO-ROUND
OF MATCHES THAT RISE BY THEMSELVES

Tip: if it won't hold, add a
drop of honey to the red end!

When you are successful with four,
try with six, eight and so on

Magical moment:
all the legs rise.

MATERIALS
MATCHES
ALUMINUM FOIL

HOW TO MAKE

1 Protect the table surface with aluminum foil.

2 Slightly shorten a match by breaking it, and place it right in the middle of a ball of aluminum foil, with the red end facing up.

3 Position four other matches in a teepee shape, around the central match, with all the red ends joined at the middle.

4 Light the red ends of the matches: as they burn, the matches will rise and will no longer touch the table.

FIRE THAT DRINKS WATER
OR AN EXPERIMENT THAT REVEALS SUBMERGED TREASURE

MATERIALS
A SHINY COIN
A WIDE, SHALLOW BOWL
SOY SAUCE
   (OR ANOTHER COLORED LIQUID)
A TEA LIGHT
A MATCH OR A LIGHTER
A GLASS

HOW TO MAKE
1 Place the coin in the dish and pour in enough soy sauce to just cover the coin.
2 Place the tea light in the puddle of liquid and light it.
3 Place a glass, upside down, over the candle: the liquid will be instantly suctioned upward due to the heat (as it burns the carbon dioxide from the air), and the coin will become visible.

Use soy sauce to create a dark pool where a treasure can be hidden.

Once the glass is placed over the heat source, the magic happens really fast! Also try it with a bigger glass.

You can see the level of dark liquid is now higher in the glass than it is in the bowl.

FAKE SNOW
❄ MADE FROM SHAVING CREAM AND CORN STARCH

HOW TO MAKE

1 Using the ends of your fingers, mix together shaving cream and corn starch in a large bowl until you end up with a substance that has a consistency that is neither too sticky nor too powdery: you now have fake snow.

2 Knead more firmly and keep adding shaving cream and corn starch until you have a uniform paste: you now have modeling clay that is very fine and soft to the touch.

MATERIALS

SHAVING CREAM
CORN STARCH
A LARGE BOWL
A PLASTICIZED WORK SURFACE

What joy — the mixture of these two textures!

And then it transforms like magic into modeling clay.

This fake snow transforms itself into modeling clay that is so fine that you can even use it to take your fingerprints or the imprint of a leaf with its delicate veins.

BETTER THAN CANDLES
FOR A BIRTHDAY CAKE

MATERIALS
A CAKE
A BOX OF MATCHES

HOW TO MAKE

1 Insert the matches into the cake — completely straight and very close together, all at the same height — to form a number or letter.

2 Light one end (for example, in the photo, the middle of the 3) and watch the flame spread instantaneously to the other matches.

When you light the middle of the 3, the flame separates in two.

The closer the matches are to one another, the faster they burn!

It's also pretty afterward.

AN EXPERIMENT WHERE A CABBAGE LEAF
CHANGES COLOR

MATERIALS
A LEAF OF CABBAGE
INK
WATER
A GLASS

HOW TO MAKE

1 Put the base of the cabbage leaf into a glass of water dyed with ink. Wait.

2 The leaf will absorb the liquid and color itself little by little. The result will be even more awesome after a few days.

This was originally a leaf of green cabbage!

99

SEPARATING THE YOLK FROM THE WHITE
WITH THE HELP OF A BOTTLE

MATERIALS
TWO EGGS
TWO BOWLS
A SMALL, EMPTY PLASTIC BOTTLE

1 Break the eggs in a bowl without breaking the yolks.

2 Position the empty bottle on top of the yolk.

100

3 Squeeze the bottle and it will suction up the yolk.

4 The yolk gets sucked up into the bottle like liquid in a syringe.

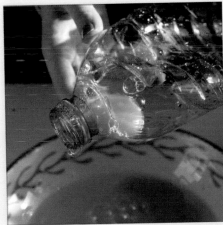

5 Tilt the bottle to retrieve only the yolk.

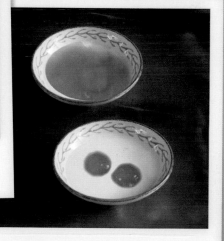

6 Slide it into the other bowl and start over.

A CANDLE MADE FROM A CLEMENTINE
WITH NO WICK OR WAX —
AND IT SMELLS GREAT

MATERIALS
A CLEMENTINE
OLIVE OIL
A SHARP KNIFE
MATCHES

HOW TO MAKE

1 Cut around the perimeter of the clementine, in the middle, but only as deep as the peel.

2 Delicately remove the pulp without damaging the two peel halves.

3 One of the halves contains a small white stem, it will serve as the wick. Pour a few drops of olive oil into the bottom of the peel to soak the stem.

4 Pierce a hole in the middle of the other half, it will be on top of the flame. You can make it round or star-shaped.

5 Light the stem and to close the clementine. Add more oil when the flame weakens.

102

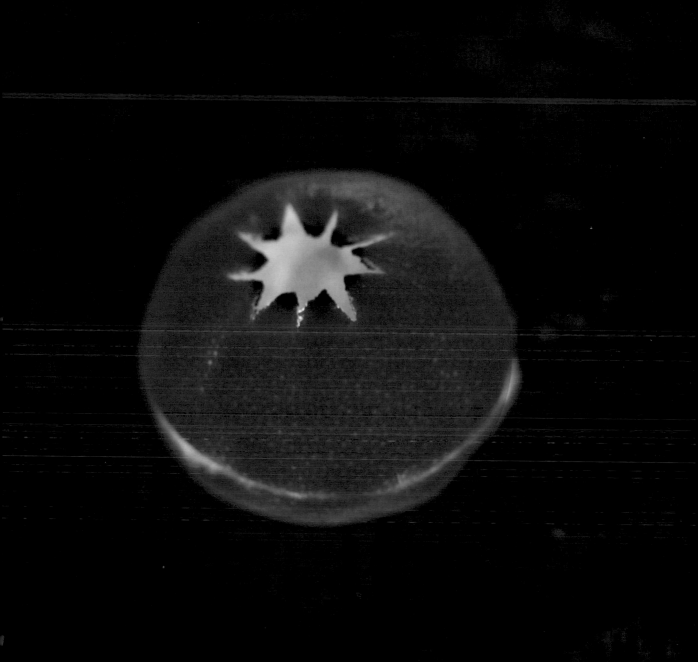

103

And you can
EAT IT!

PLAYMOBIL® ICE POPS
THAT CAN STAND UP

MATERIALS
ICE POP MOLDS
SOME PLAYMOBIL OR LEGO FIGURINES
SOME DRINKS
   (FRUIT JUICE, SODAS, OR WATER AND SYRUP)

HOW TO MAKE

1 Wash the figurines well and place them upside down into the molds so that their legs stick out (they will sink on their own).

2 Fill the molds with cold drinks of your choice, and place them in the freezer.

3 Leave in the freezer at least 4 hours and then unmold them. If needed, you can run some warm water over the molds to help free the ice pops. Eat them quickly!

HONEY PANCAKES
SHAPED LIKE BEES

INGREDIENTS
3 EGGS
1⅝ CUPS (375 ML) WHEAT FLOUR
1 CUP (250 ML) MILK
2 TBSP (30 ML) POWDERED SUGAR
½ PACKAGE OF YEAST
POWDERED CHOCOLATE
HONEY

HOW TO MAKE

1 Separate the egg whites from the yolks and beat the whites until they're stiff and peaks form.

2 In a separate bowl, stir together the yolks, sugar, flour and yeast. Add in the milk a little at a time, and then fold in the egg whites.

3 Place a little of the batter into another bowl and mix in some powdered chocolate.

4 Heat a medium-sized pan over medium heat. Using an eyedropper (like the type provided with children's medication), draw the outline and the stripes of the bees with the chocolate batter. Allow to cook for a minute or two.

5 Using a small spoon, cover these drawings with the white batter.

6 Flip over the pancake as soon as bubbles start forming in the batter and cook for a few more moments on the other side.

7 To create the hive, cook some round and crescent-shaped pancakes of varying sizes, and stack them on the plate. Serve with honey.

The trick is to use an eyedropper to create the detailed drawings.

It's important to create the bees in two steps: first using the dark batter, then the white.

CHOCOLATE CROISSANTS
ROLLED IN 5 MINUTES

INGREDIENTS
A ROLL OF FILO PASTRY
CHOCOLATE SPREAD

HOW TO MAKE

1 Unroll the filo pastry and cut it into eight equal parts.

2 Put chocolate spread onto each triangle.

3 Roll them up to a point, then stretch them out a little to give them the shape of a croissant.

4 Bake them in a 350°F (180°C) oven for 15 minutes, checking them every minute or so toward the end of the baking time.

COCKTAIL DECORATIONS
MADE OF APPLES FOR THE KIDS' HAPPY HOUR

You can make four big leaves from one apple.

INGREDIENTS
A GREEN APPLE
A RED APPLE

HOW TO MAKE

1 To create the large green leaf, cut a small slit on the side of the green apple.

2 Cut two bigger slits, parallel to the first one, and so forth, as thinly as possible.

3 The last step is to slide the pieces one on top of the other to stagger them: the pectin in the apples will cause the slices to stick to each other very well.

4 To create the red apple flower, cut small notches all around the stem.

5 Cut off the upper third of the apple horizontally and cut out the shapes of petals around the notches.

The flower looks best if you choose an apple with a stem.

A BALL FOREST
WITH SURPRISES INSIDE

INGREDIENTS
CREAM CHEESE
CHERRY TOMATOES
GRAPES
OLIVES
SPICES
FRESH FINE HERBS, CHOPPED
EDIBLE SEEDS
  (SESAME, POPPY, FLAX)
TWIGS

HOW TO MAKE

1 Cover the cherry tomatoes, grapes and olives with cream cheese.

2 Roll the balls into the spices, fresh chopped herbs or seeds – whatever you prefer.

3 Insert the twigs into the balls and serve this forest as an appetizer or part of a buffet.

A LANDSCAPE CRACKER
YOU'RE ALLOWED TO BREAK

The landscape before baking.
Later, we take out the hammer!

INGREDIENTS
1 TBSP (15 ML) BUTTER
A BUNCH OF FRESH BASIL
2 CUPS (500 ML) FLOUR
1 CUP (250 ML) SOUR CREAM
1 TSP (15 ML) POWDERED SUGAR
SALT
CUMIN
PARCHMENT PAPER
SOME MILK

HOW TO MAKE

1 Remove the butter from the refrigerator and let it soften. Preheat the oven to 350°F (180°C).

2 Select the basil leaves that look the best and leave them on their stems to create the landscape. Chop the rest.

3 Mix the flour, sour cream, sugar, chopped basil, salt and cumin in a mixing bowl. Knead until you have a uniform ball of dough.

4 Roll out the dough as thinly as possible on parchment paper and dab a little milk onto the dough with your fingers.

5 Place the leaves of basil in such a way that they create a bouquet or a landscape. The milk will help the leaves adhere to the dough.

6 Bake in the oven for approximately 15 minutes, checking for doneness toward the end of baking time. As soon as the edges of the cracker begin to brown, take it out of the oven.

7 Let cool and serve whole. Your guests can break off a piece when the appetizers are served!

CHEESE LOLLIPOPS
GUARANTEED TO BE SUGAR-FREE

INGREDIENTS AND MATERIALS
A VARIETY OF CHEESES
   (PARMESAN, GRUYERE, GOUDA, MOZZARELLA, ETC.), GRATED
HERBS, SPICES AND SEEDS
WOODEN SKEWERS OR POPSICLE STICKS

HOW TO MAKE
1 Form small mounds of grated cheese in a frying pan.

2 Add decorative elements (herbs, spices or seeds) as well as a skewer or Popsicle stick.

3 Let melt in the pan. Wait until the lollipops have cooled and hardened before presenting them upright.

119

A MOBILE MADE OF CHEESE DOILIES
TO EAT WITH NO HANDS

INGREDIENTS AND MATERIALS
A ROLL OF SHORT CRUST PASTRY
PARCHMENT PAPER
GRATED CHEESE
SPICES OF YOUR CHOOSING
THREAD
A TREE BRANCH

HOW TO MAKE

1 Create small frames with the short crust pastry. Place them on the parchment paper.

2 Sprinkle them with a bit of grated cheese and your choice of spices.

3 Bake in a 350°F (180°C) oven for approximately 10 minutes.

4 When they are baked and have cooled down, tie them with thread to a suspended tree branch. (In the photo, a very thin metal wire was used, but it can be dangerous if children bite into the doilies too forcefully.)

121

A BABYBEL® FAMILY
OR SCULPTURES YOU CAN EAT

• • •

Baby girl

Baby lady

Baby balaclava

INGREDIENTS AND MATERIALS
A BLACK STRAW
A PRECISE CUTTING TOOL
SOME MINI BABYBEL
BLACK SESAME SEEDS
SCISSORS

HOW TO MAKE
1 Cut out very short segments from the straw: they will be used to create the contour of the eyes.

2 Cut out wax from the cheese, as shown.

3 Push in straw segments and sesame seeds to create the eyes.

Baby chic

Baby umbrella

Crazy Baby

Baby fish

Baby bug

Baby with goggles

123

SPAGHETTI HOT DOGS
A FOOD EXPERIMENT

—

INGREDIENTS
SPAGHETTI NOODLES
HOT DOGS
A POT OF WATER

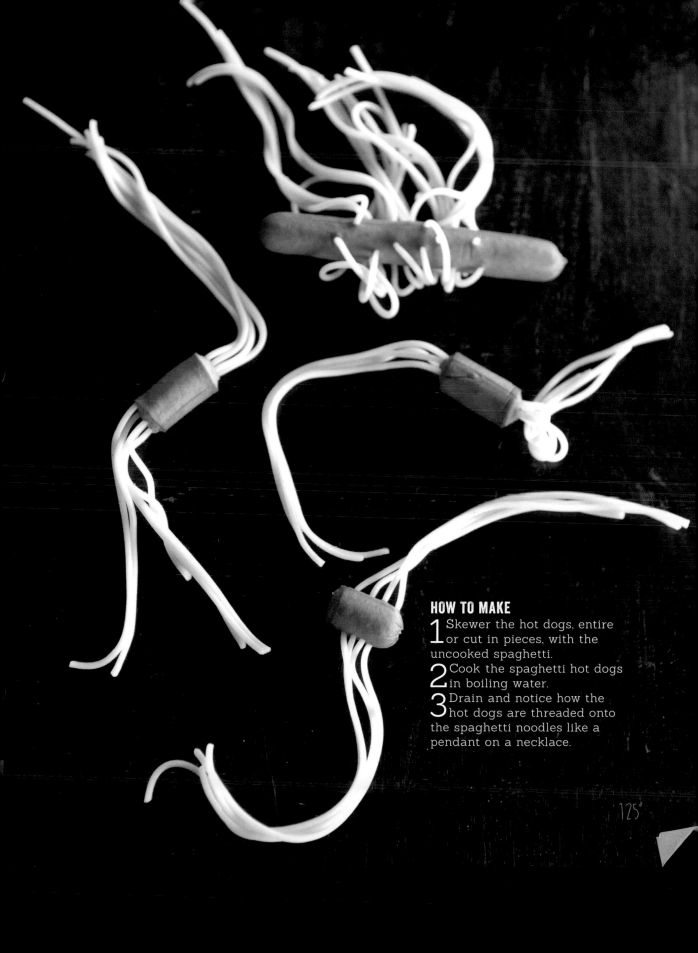

HOW TO MAKE

1 Skewer the hot dogs, entire or cut in pieces, with the uncooked spaghetti.

2 Cook the spaghetti hot dogs in boiling water.

3 Drain and notice how the hot dogs are threaded onto the spaghetti noodles like a pendant on a necklace.

A FORTIFIED CASTLE CAKE
MADE ALMOST ENTIRELY OF CHOCOLATE

INGREDIENTS
THREE BROWNIES MEASURING APPROXIMATELY 8×8 INCHES
   (20×20 CM)
TOOTHPICKS
48 SANDWICH COOKIES, LIKE OREOS
FIVE CHOCOLATE–COATED BISCUIT STICKS, LIKE POCKY
A HALF SHEET OF CHOCOLATE SQUARES
CANDY

HOW TO MAKE

1 Cut two brownies in half to form the four walls. Cut some small cubes out of the third brownie; these will be used to create the top of the fortified walls of the castle. Secure the cubes with toothpicks.

2 From one of the walls, cut out the shape of the door and insert three chocolate-coated biscuit sticks into it to create the fortified gate.

3 Raise the four walls as well as the cookie towers in the four corners. Use the sheet of chocolate and two chocolate-coated biscuit sticks and place to act as the drawbridge. Fill the castle with candy.

A MOON CAKE
WITH LYCHEE CRATERS

HOW TO MAKE

1 If you are using a metal or Pyrex bowl, wrap it in aluminum foil so it will be easier to unmold later (parchment paper does not work well on a spherical shape).

2 Make the cake batter that you've selected – a store-bought cake mix works well. Make sure it's a rising cake. Pour the prepared batter into the mold and bake the cake. When the cake has finished baking, unmold it, turn it upside down and let it cool completely.

3 Prepare the icing by mixing the cream cheese, lemon juice and icing sugar. Ice the cake.

4 Create holes in the icing using the cork. You can also pat the icing with a flat spatula to create an irregular effect like in the photo.

5 Cut a few lychees in half to obtain a small ring and small dome with each fruit. Place them on the icing to represent the craters and the hills. Finish decorating using the small white candies.

INGREDIENTS AND MATERIALS

A METAL SALAD BOWL OR CAKE MOLD
ALUMINUM FOIL
A CLASSIC CAKE RECIPE
½ CUP (125 ML) SPREADABLE CREAM CHEESE
JUICE OF HALF A LEMON
½ CUP (125 ML) ICING SUGAR
A CORK
A CAN OF LYCHEES IN SYRUP
SMALL WHITE CANDIES

You can use a store-bought cake mix.

The theme lends itself especially well to sparklers.

Gagarin

Laika

129

A CAMPFIRE CAKE
WITH MARSHMALLOW EMBERS

INGREDIENTS AND MATERIALS

A CAKE
SOME MARSHMALLOWS
BREAD STICKS
POWDERED SUGAR
PARCHMENT PAPER
PEBBLES

HOW TO MAKE

1 Put some powdered sugar in a frying pan to create caramel. Cook on medium heat without handling until the sugar melts and browns.

2 When the caramel has liquefied, spread it on parchment paper using a flexible spatula; be sure to leave some irregular edges. Let it harden.

3 Skewer the marshmallows with a fork or skewer stick over the flame from a fire, candle or gas stove.

4 Arrange the bread sticks on the cake to look like a pile of wood. Add the marshmallows to look like charcoal.

5 Break up pieces of the cooled caramel and arrange them to look like flames on the cake.

6 Place pebbles all around the cake to complete the campfire look.

The caramel. You can also melt candy in the oven as a substitute.

CAGES MADE OF SPUN SUGAR
TO DECORATE A CAKE

INGREDIENTS AND MATERIALS
POWDERED SUGAR
A FRYING PAN
A FORK
A BIG BOWL
PARCHMENT PAPER
FEROCIOUS ANIMALS

HOW TO MAKE

1 Make caramel by pouring powdered sugar into a frying pan. Let it melt on its own without handling.

2 Cover the upside down bowl with parchment paper. (If the bowl is small, you can simply coat the outside surface with a little oil.)

3 Dip a fork into the caramel and create caramel threads on the bowl, ensuring they are intertwined.

4 As soon as the caramel is dry, unmold and carefully place this sugary cage over the animals.

133

A MOUNTAIN CAKE
AND ITS CLIMBERS

If using store-bought brownies, you can use the cardboard wrapper to create the cone.

MATERIALS

THIN CARDBOARD
ADHESIVE TAPE
ALUMINUM FOIL
TOOTHPICKS

SEVERAL BROWNIES
POWDERED CHOCOLATE
SMALL PLASTIC SOLDIERS
A BOX CUTTER
SOME STRING

HOW TO MAKE

1 Form a non-symmetrical cone with the cardboard and hold it together with the adhesive tape. Cover the cone with crumpled aluminum foil.

2 Insert the toothpicks into the cone. Once they're all inserted, place hand-broken brownie pieces (don't cut them with a knife) onto the toothpicks. Sprinkle with powdered chocolate.

3 Cut off the weapons from the plastic soldiers with your box cutter and join the soldiers together two-by-two by tying string around their waists. Spread out the soldiers all around the mountain, alternating those who are climbing and those who are spotting.

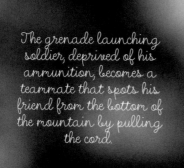

The grenade launching soldier, deprived of his ammunition, becomes a teammate that spots his friend from the bottom of the mountain by pulling the cord.

Part of the fun is figuring out how to turn soldier moves into mountain-climbing moves.

Crawling soldiers
become perfect climbers
once they're placed
vertically instead.

THE PHASES OF THE MOON
MADE FROM SANDWICH COOKIES

MATERIALS
SEVEN SANDWICH COOKIES
A SHARP KNIFE

HOW TO MAKE

1 Open up the cookies without damaging the cream filling

2 Put aside the half of the cookie without filling on it to create the nights without a moon, and the half with the filling untouched to create the full moon.

3 Using the knife, scrape the filling from the other cookies to represent the different phases of the moon.

new moon

waning crescent

waxing crescent

last quarter

first quarterr

waning gibbous

waxing gibbous

full moon

WHAT YOU'LL DISCOVER IN
HOW TO AMAZE YOUR DAUGHTER...

an experiment with magic milk

a carousel cake

a rubbery egg that lost its shell

an effervescent experiment

a jellyfish in a bottle

little radish mice

a laundry jug house

a tablecloth that becomes a tent

wax bubble candle holders

141

THEMATIC INDEX
SELECTED

ALPHABETICAL INDEX

THANK YOUS

Thank you to my son **Félix** and my daughter **Avril** for their help on numerous pages and for their perpetual enthusiasm. Thank you to the other children who posed: **Micha, Aloïs, Raphaël, Simon** and **Maïa**.

Thank you to my mother **Bernadette,** who still amazes me at my age: she made the teepee, the shark pencil case, the jungle cave, the small doors for the electrical outlets and the alphabetical shelf.

Thank you to **Corine** who helped and supported me throughout, who drew on the baby photos with **Anna's** help as well as made the ghosts and the cardboard tree house.

Thank you to **Loran,** who made the Mölkky game and the peanut trophy, and who also helped with the photos.

Thank you also to **Yves** and to **Léa** for their contribution to the photo shoots.

Text, photos and layout: Raphaële Vidaling
Cover creation: Marina Delranc
Photo engraving: Peggy Huynh-Quan-Suu
Book produced by Copyright

144